Touch

....What do you feel?

Library of Congress Cataloging-in-Publication Data

Wood, Nicholas, (date)
  Touch—what do you feel? / by Nicholas Wood; illustrated by
Lynne Willey.
    p.   cm.—(First science)
  Summary: Explores the world of touch, examining how it works and
what it tells us about our surroundings.
    ISBN 0-8167-2126-2 (lib. bdg.)   ISBN 0-8167-2127-0 (pbk.)
    1. Touch—Juvenile literature. [1. Touch. 2. Senses and
sensation.] I. Willey, Lynne, ill. II. Title.
QP451.W66 1991
612.8 '8—dc20   90-10925

Published by Troll Associates, Mahwah, New Jersey 07430

Printed in the U.S.A.

10 9 8 7 6 5 4 3 2 1

Touch
...What do you feel?

Written by
Nicholas Wood

Illustrated by
Lynne Willey

Troll Associates

Look at these objects.
How do you think they will feel
if you touch them?

Now run your fingers
over the pictures.
How do they really feel?

4

The pebbles look
round and smooth.
The rock looks
hard and sharp
along the edges.
The egg carton looks bumpy.
But they all *FEEL*
like a piece of paper.

5

People love touching things.
It helps them learn
about what's around them.
But sometimes touching
isn't allowed.

Some animals like
to be touched.
Cats like to be stroked.
And dogs sometimes lie
on their backs
and let you tickle
their tummies.
But always ask someone
before you stroke or pat
a strange animal.

When two ponies meet,
they sometimes rub noses.

Some insects have feelers
called antennae,
so they can feel if
there's anything in the way.
Lobsters also have antennae,
to feel their way along
the bottom of the sea.

An elephant may touch things
with his trunk. He wants to know
if this bridge is safe to cross.

Some things feel good
to touch.
A lamb feels warm and soft.

But some things feel bad.

When you walk on the beach,
the hot sand can hurt
your feet. Or broken seashells
can give you a cut.

It's best to wear shoes
on the beach
to protect your feet.

When we touch something,
we feel it against our skin.
Inside our skin
there are
lots of little feelers,
called nerve endings.
Some feel heat.
Some feel cold.
Some feel pain.
Some feel when something is
pressing against them.

Nerves are like wires.
They carry messages
from the nerve endings
to the brain.

Some parts of the body
feel things better
than other parts
because there are
more nerve endings
in the skin.
Try touching your face
with the tip of a soft brush.
Now touch your arm.
Which part
do you think
has more nerve endings?

There are no nerve endings
in your hair or your nails.
Try touching these
with a brush.
What do you feel?

There are lots of nerve endings
in your fingertips,
and by moving your fingers
you can feel
the shape of something
in your hand.
Is it round or square?
Long or short?

By holding something,
you may be able
to guess its weight.

I'll have some apples
for an apple pie.

You can feel
a piece of fruit
or a vegetable
to find out
if it's ripe
and ready to eat.

This melon feels too hard.
It's not ripe yet.
This melon feels too soft.
It may be bad.
This melon feels just right.
Not too hard.
And not too soft.

19

Every time you touch something,
you leave a mark.
The mark left by your fingertip
is called a fingerprint.
If you've been doing something messy,
you can see your fingerprints.
If your hands are clean,
you can't see your fingerprints,
but they're still there.

Detectives use special powder
which sticks to fingerprints
and shows where they are.
Let's see.
Who's been touching
things in here?
A detective would match up
the fingerprints.
He will soon know
who picked up the cup.

Blind people have
more need to touch things
than people who can see.
Books for blind people
are made with bumps
instead of letters,
so that blind people
can feel the words.
This way of printing
with bumps
is called Braille.

Braille was invented
by a man named Louis Braille.
He was blind, so he knew
how useful his invention
would be.

What does it feel like
to read Braille?
Get some paper and press
it against something
hard and bumpy.
Can you feel the bumps
on the paper? That's
what Braille feels like.
In Braille, there's a
different pattern
of bumps
or raised dots
for each letter
of the alphabet.

L
I
K
E
T
H
I
S

When blind people
read Braille,
they use
both hands.
The left hand finds
the beginning of the line,
while the right hand
reads the words.
Can you see
what words
this person
is reading?

You can put
different things
in a bag,
and ask a friend
to guess
what they are
by touching them.
A pencil.
A button.
An apple.
A sponge.
They all feel different.

But be careful.
Some things hurt.

People don't like pain,
but it can be useful
because it tells us
when something is wrong.

If a pain is very sharp,
our body may react
before the message reaches our brain.
This is called a reflex action.

1) Hand touches something hot.
   Nerve endings feel pain.

2) Message goes quickly to
   arm muscles.
   Hand jumps back.

3) Message reaches brain.

Yowee! That's hot.

Some things are too hot
to touch.
You'd better wear gloves.

He's wearing
oven gloves –
he's baking a pie.

Come on in.
It's time for dinner.

Some things are too sharp to touch.
She's wearing gardening gloves —
she's planting
a prickly rose.

Some touches, like hugging,
make us feel warm and safe.
Some touches tell us
when things are too hot or too cold.
But touching things is an important way
of learning about our world.